20
INSPIRING
TRUE STORIES
FOR AMAZING GIRLS LIKE ME

Extraordinary Tales of Brave Women
Who Redefined American History

MADELYN LEE

"I alone cannot change the world,
but I can cast a stone across the
waters to create many ripples."

– Mother Teresa

TABLE OF CONTENTS

INTRODUCTION

A ll the women in this book are extraordinary.
But all of them are ordinary, too.
The above quote from Mother Teresa is about creating change like a gently lapping wave. Many lapping waves can become a rising tide that goes from low to high in moments—and it all begins with a single drop of water.

Change is like that.

Girls who change the world are like that, too.

All the women presented here are extraordinary for what they achieved in their lives, but they're even more super-mega-extraordinary because of the change they brought out in others!

All of these women are pioneers.

All of them are heroines.

All of the women in this book were once young girls like you—looking for inspiration in the world around them.

Life is inspiring, and these women are, too. When you look for ways to enjoy your life and help others, you'll find that you will become inspiring, too.

Who knows—maybe I'll be writing a book about you one day!

I certainly hope so. That's why I'm writing this book now! It's for girls like you, girls like me, and everyone else (even boys... but shhhh, they might get jealous of how awesome these super girls are)!

If you're looking for action, adventure, inspiration, courage, bravery, strength, and stories about overcoming fears, you're in great company.

Ready to meet them?

Let's go!

A fun note: Throughout the book, you will find a bunch of activities and fun questions for you to answer!

Okay, are you ready to meet everyone?

1
AMELIA EARHART

Pioneering Aviator | Writer
Conquering Woman of the Skies
July 24, 1897 - Disappeared July 2, 1937
Declared dead January 5th, 1939
Atchinson, Kansas

"Women, like men, should try to do the impossible.
And when they fail, their failure should be
a challenge to others."

Whooooooshhhhhh!

The wind bellowed like a brewing hurricane as Amelia's plane bounced around in the blowing gale like a kite. She was afraid, but tried not to be. She wasn't going to lose her cool—not when she was so close to finishing! And not after 14 hours of continuous flying crossing the Atlantic Ocean, from Canada to the United Kingdom!

If she lost her cool, it would only prove what those crazy journalists had suggested—that women couldn't be pilots!

Amelia's leather gloves squeaked in the cold air as she tightened her grip on the yoke (the airplane's "steering wheel"). She wished she were warmer. Her hands and bones were freezing. She also wished she had more fuel in her tank. But wishing accomplished nothing. It was only her determination that would finish this flight!

Amelia looked down at the ocean below her. It was a long way down. The dark water was gray and murky, and waves crashed into each other in foamy white sprays of excitement.

Amelia's desire to succeed was strong. She refused to feel lonely up in the air, or to give up. She couldn't wait to feel satisfied and proud. She would prove that she was just as capable as any other pilot.

But over the next hour, doubt crept into her heart. The excitement and adrenaline turned into fear and bad thoughts. She became cold again. She was also a little bit afraid that she wouldn't find land.

The fuel gauge went ever lower, and soon she doubted if she'd even read the map right! But Amelia knew she had read all her gauges correctly. She was just doubting herself.

Wait...was she seeing what she thought she was seeing?

Fishing boats? A port?

Land?

Have you ever been afraid of doing something exciting? Sometimes nervousness and excitement can feel the same as fear, like butterflies fluttering in our chest. Have you felt that and pushed on?

Well, Amelia did!

On May 21st, 1932, Amelia Earhart became the first woman to fly across the Atlantic Ocean. It took a lot of bravery to do what she did. Many people didn't think women could fly, but she proved them wrong!

Amelia took off in Canada, with the entire world doubting women pilots, and landed in Ireland, proving that they were just as skilled as any male pilot.

They were equal!

But, that's not all... While we all know Amelia Earhart for her fearless and record-breaking flights in aviation, this female pilot who conquered the flying world didn't even originally like planes!

Amelia loved the *idea* of flying—and later loved writing books about her flying adventures—but originally she wasn't that impressed with the first plane she saw. She thought it was a heap of junk! Talk about a let down.

While the idea of a plane didn't land with Amelia at first, adventure always had. As a kid, she loved building ramps in her backyard and flying down them on her sled (even when they didn't work). She didn't give up when those ramps failed. For Amelia, failures were chances to improve! That was something she thought about for the rest of her life.

It was Amelia Earhart's way of seeing failure that took her from humble beginnings to heights most people never imagined. She made her life an adventure, and it was the adventures that gave her opportunities to break expectations and open doors for other girls to fly through.

That's not to say it was always easy. It wasn't. A lot of men had the silly idea that women couldn't fly planes. Some didn't even want to let women try! These rejections would hurt Amelia's feelings, but she didn't let them stop her. Instead, she proved everyone wrong and flew her way to freedom.

Flying wasn't the only way Amelia felt free. When she wasn't flying among the clouds, she would fly between the covers of a good book. This provided the same excitement as flying in real life—it was as if she were discovering new worlds and lands. Throughout her life, Amelia was most comfortable with a book and following her curiosity.

It was Amelia's curiosity that made her such a great explorer. Whenever something went wrong on a trip or adventure, she didn't see it as a failure, but rather a challenge and an opportunity to solve a problem. And when things went right, Amelia proved to the world that all women deserve to be in the skies and chasing their dreams, no matter how high they flew!

Amelia was always up to fun adventures and following her curiosity! Here are five fun facts about her:

1. Amelia Earhart's nickname as a kid was "Meelie."
2. Amelia once built her own rollercoaster! Okay, she had help from her uncle—and the whole thing didn't work—but she had a lot of fun building it.
3. Amelia was the 16th woman to get her flying license.
4. Amelia was the first woman to fly an autogiro (autogiros are like a helicopter crossed with a plane).
5. Amelia also designed women's clothes that were practical to fly in.

2
PURA BELPRÉ

Librarian | Spreader of Dreams
Wise Woman of Words
February 2, 1899 - July 1, 1982
Cidra, Puerto Rico

"To appreciate the present, one must have a knowledge of the past... To know where we go, we must know from where we came..."

Slash!
The tiger's claws swiped in front of Pura and she stumbled back. The claws of Shere Khan clicked and clacked as he paced back and forth. The proud king was readying to pounce. With a quick jump he—

Pura snapped the cover shut and placed *The Jungle Book* back on the shelf. The library on 135th street in Harlem was quiet for a Wednesday afternoon. Pura felt like a little girl among all these books and stories she'd loved as a child. She was so excited, she didn't know what to read first.

She wanted to read *La Cucarachita Martina,* or maybe *La Puerta Chiriante.* Pura didn't mind—she would read whatever she found. She just had to find the section with Puerto Rican stories, first.

Her excitement was building with each step, but by the time she'd shuffled all the way to the end of the aisle, her heart had gone from excitement to doubt. Soon it was full of sadness.

There weren't any Puerto Rican stories. There also wasn't a single book in Spanish. The magical lands she'd known as a child were nowhere to be found!

Pura thought of her abuela (grandmother). If she couldn't see the stories, that didn't mean they were forgotten. If she'd learned one thing from the stories of her heritage, it was that if you wanted to see something happen, then sometimes you had to make it happen yourself!

Which fairy tales and stories do you like? Are there any stories about princesses or animals that you like and can see clearly? Were they read to you, or did you read them yourself?

Imagine a library without any of your favorite stories or characters.

That's what Pura Belpré found when she was browsing the library in New York while visiting her sister. She had loved the stories her abuela told her as a child, but now she felt even more homesick not finding them.

The determination to see her country's stories among the books of New York's Library system inspired Pura to become a librarian. What's more, she was the first Puerto Rican woman to be hired in the public system. 1921 was a momentous year, indeed!

Pura started a bilingual storytime, and brought Puerto Rican and many other Latinx folktales to life in Spanish and English with the help of puppets. Kids loved it! The popularity of the tales spread like wildfire. Soon, an entire generation was learning the stories she'd loved as a child.

But, that's not all... While it was Pura's search for the books of her childhood that started her adventure, when she finished her librarian studies and moved to southwest Harlem for her next role, her sharing went to a whole new level.

Pura became an advocate for all things related to Puerto Rican folk and fairy tale history! She brought original books from Puerto Rico and shared them with the community. Then, she rewrote these stories in English so other people could enjoy them, too. Finally, she went and did it again with other Latinx countries! She loved for Latinx people to learn about their heritage, and wanted them to have the ability to understand it, so she started a language and reading class, as well. The 115th street library became a home for all Latinx adults and children in New York, forever changing the lives of generations to come.

When Pura met her husband, a very talented musician named Clarence Cameron White, she could finally dedicate all her time to writing. But writing wasn't easy—not everyone liked her stories! And some people didn't like that Latinx people had come to America for a better life. Whether because of the languages she spoke or the color of her skin, Pura sometimes faced hard times.

It was a good thing she was fearless! She just wanted to share her culture and history. The stories her abuela had lovingly told her inspired her to keep going. In the end, Pura's work inspired generations of children and adults to read stories about themselves and their histories.

Now, her dedication lives on through the Pura Belpré Award. This is an honor granted to Latinx authors and illustrators each year who write fantastic stories about Latinx cultures!

As Pura said, the most important thing about knowing how to move forward is understanding where we've come from.

Do you know your heritage? In what creative and fun ways do you express it?

1. Are there any dances that symbolize your ancestry?
2. What about music? Do you sing at the top of your lungs with your family when you're all together?
3. Food can express culture, too. Are there any special dishes you enjoy cooking with your family?
4. Do you have any clothes or customs that you celebrate?
5. What fun activity could you do to discover more of your ancestry?

3
ELIZABETH COCHRANE SEAMAN

Investigative Journalist | Record-Breaker
Princess of the Printed Word

May 5, 1864 - January 27, 1922

Burrell Township, Pennsylvania

"I have never written a word that did not come from my heart. I never shall."

Shhhlump!

Elizabeth dropped into the chair with an exhausted sigh. Her feet ached from the cold snow and her pink hands were scrubbed raw from the stinky laundry. In fact, she could still smell the stinky laundry on her skin...eww!

But there was so much more to do. She still had to help her mother cook.

All Elizabeth really wanted to do was curl up with a good book. That sounded fantastic. But she didn't know how she'd ever find time to read—let alone write!

Just thinking about everything she had to do made her sad. Then, she remembered the stinky factory owner who had refused to give her a job because she was a girl. She became frustrated again.

Elizabeth loved writing and telling stories. That's what she really wanted to do. Her words gave her a voice, and she wanted to do good with her words.

Noticing yesterday's newspaper on the table, Elizabeth frowned. A headline from the *Pittsburgh Dispatch* stood out.

"What Girls Are Good For?!"

Her jaw dropped as she read, then she stomped into the kitchen in a rage. "This editor believes women shouldn't work!" she said to her mother. "We're not good enough for the workplace, we're not fit enough to run a business, all we're good for is having children and doing housework!"

Elizabeth's cheeks burned and tears of rage fell. The hurt in her chest made her feel small and insignificant. Women were capable of so much more!

"What are you going to do, then?" her mother asked.

A heartbeat passed. "I'm going to write a letter!"

Have you ever felt busy and tired like Elizabeth? Her passion to speak up, even when she was tired, energized Elizabeth and made the greatest change in her life!

Elizabeth wrote her letter. She poured all her frustrations into it and posted it the next day. Two days later, someone from the newspaper wanted to meet her! An editor named George Madden was so impressed that he wanted to give her a job. But women weren't allowed to publish with their real names in newspapers in 1885, so George hadn't realized who she was. Regardless, 20-year-old Elizabeth Cochrane stepped forward and her life changed forever.

What a change it was!

Soon, Elizabeth was writing as a reporter named Nellie Bly. And she was doing good with her words. She wrote about the horrible work conditions girls and women faced in factories. She talked about how owners were refusing to pay them equal money.

The *Pittsburgh Dispatch* started getting lots of complaints about her articles, so Elizabeth was told to move on. However, she took that as a compliment!

At 21 years of age, Elizabeth wasn't finished with her writing career. Having grown up in a poor household with 14 other siblings, she knew what it was like to not have a voice, so she went in search of people who were voiceless and needed their stories told.

From the unfairness happening in Mexico in the late 1800s to re-enacting Jules Vernes' novel *Around the World in 80 Days* by traveling the world herself (in only 72 days!), Elizabeth used her platform to tell the public about the world. In the process, she helped invent stunt journalism, which is a form of journalism where the writer has a big adventure and writes about it—or, as you'll soon see, goes undercover!

Elizabeth had heard about the terrors women were facing in a nearby mental hospital. Women were being treated in scary and frightening ways to "cure" their problems, and once Elizabeth found out, she was determined to expose it.

With the help of a newspaper, Elizabeth went undercover. She stayed up all night and pretended to rave like a madwoman. Once she was admitted to the hospital, she spent 10 days enduring frightening treatments.

When she got out, she wrote a story for the newspaper that horrified the citizens of New York. They demanded that the hospital change and treat women fairly.

But, that's not all... Elizabeth's life as a reporter was quite busy, but when she met her husband, Robert, she settled down. She spent her time writing fiction stories and working with her husband in his manufacturing plant. But then, in the early 1900s, Robert became sick and passed away. While Elizabeth was sad, she didn't have time to grieve, because she was now the head of manufacturing and inventing at the factory! It was an exciting and scary new adventure that helped her feel close to her husband, even after he was gone.

Elizabeth was determined to do things differently with her factory. As a reporter, she had seen the horrible working conditions a lot of people had to endure. Elizabeth decided she would be generous to her staff. She took care of them and gave them health benefits. Considering how a lot of factories were run at the time, she was a trailblazer in doing so. Unfortunately, her kindness was taken advantage of by accountants and ill-intentioned staff, and she soon became bankrupt. The world wasn't ready for factory owners like her.

So Elizabeth returned to what she'd always loved—writing. Her fearlessness hadn't changed one bit! Soon, she was writing about the women's suffrage movement and World War I. She was the first female reporter to write from the Eastern Front.

Over the years, she continued using her words to do good—leveraging the superpower she had always possessed in order to make the world a better place.

Do you want to try writing? Here are five writing prompts to get you started!

1. Today, I had fun doing_____. It made me feel_____. The best part was_____.
2. Today, I was frustrated because_____. It made me feel_____. The worst part was_____.
3. Today, I was excited for_____ because I like_____. By the end, I_____.
4. Today, I was sad because_____. It made me feel_____. What cheered me up, though, was_____.
5. Today, I imagined I was a _____ tree. I felt so_____, and imagined that I looked like_____.

4
ANNIE OAKLEY

Sharpshooter | America's First Female Superstar
Gal of Dedication & Practice
August 13, 1860 - November 3 , 1926
Darke County, Ohio

"Aim at the high mark and you will hit it..."

"Take aim!"

The air was cold on that Thanksgiving Day in 1875. Annie Oakley stood with her gun, ready to shoot. She breathed carefully and didn't take her eye off the target. In her eyes, it began to turn into a giant saucer plate, zooming at her. It was just waiting for her to pull the trigger.

Long months in cold winters and the need to provide for her family had taught 15-year-old Annie how to shoot. She inhaled slightly and squeezed the trigger.

The last target exploded and Annie grinned. She'd won.

A man 10 years older than her stood in awe. His mistake on the last round had created the opportunity for her to shoot for the win.

"You're pretty cool under pressure," he said.

"Thank you," Annie replied.

"Where'd you learn to shoot?"

The trees of Darke County descended around Annie and the freezing winter pulled her into a crystallized memory. The woods were crisp and the air had chilled her lungs as she breathed—it sent shivers down her spine just thinking about it now.

"Well, you know, shooting is all practice. These targets are easy. What's hard is hitting a deer as it runs away and you're really hungry."

The man chuckled. "So, your father taught you to hunt."

"No, sir. I taught myself." Annie left out the fact that she was a Quaker, and that using a weapon was actually against her religion. Teaching herself to shoot had been an act of desperation.

The man's jaw dropped.

People began congratulating Annie. Men whistled and laughed in joy at the sight of the young woman defeating the marksman. But the man Annie had beaten still stood in awe. Annie's cheeks flushed red. She would've felt embarrassed for him if it wasn't for the fact that she'd just won $100!

Have you ever performed an impressive feat in front of people? If so, what was it? How did things go? Were you proud of the fact that you did it, or even that you simply tried?

Annie's real name was Phoebe Ann Mosey. She was only 15 years old when she stepped up to the challenge that day. She didn't know that shooting would soon become her career, but she did know that she was good at it—so she decided to have a go!

But even with Annie's calmness while shooting, she was still nervous. She hadn't always been the best shot, which is why she'd practiced so much.

What Annie didn't know was that the man she had been competing against was really good. His name was Frank E. Butler, and everyone had expected him to win. But this is where Annie's dedication to practicing her skills came through. Not only did she win, she impressed Frank Butler! In fact, it was Frank who told Annie she could make money with her marksmanship skills. He then made her part of his own act (they even fell in love, too!).

Before that competition, Annie had already made a name for herself with her shooting in Darke County. She'd told the truth when she'd said that she'd taught herself. Annie had learned to shoot when her family had no food or money to buy food. She took her father's rifle off the mantle and practiced in the woods until she was a shooting queen!

But, that's not all... Annie soon became America's first female superstar. She was so good at shooting that she was offered bigger shows with greater responsibilities! But it all began with Frank (who was now her husband!). Their act together had gotten people talking. Everyone wanted to see the wonderful Annie Oakley shooting and performing with her incredible skills.

A man called William Cody soon discovered Annie. If Frank had been impressed with her abilities, then William was gobsmacked. William ran a show called *Buffalo Bill's Wild West*, and it traveled around the world.

He wanted Annie to join his crew.

Annie said yes, and they began touring all over Europe and the United Kingdom. She performed for kings and queens and impressed lots of people as she shot cigars from her husband's hands, split playing cards, and even split apples in mid-air!

Annie was passionate about her skill and always encouraged others to learn how to shoot. Some say she taught over 15,000 women how to shoot in her lifetime. Annie thought it was important that a lady knew how to protect herself. Also, it was quite fun!

But being Annie Oakley the Sharpshooter wasn't always easy. Not everyone thought her lifestyle was proper, and some people told her this in harsh words. Fortunately, she paid them no mind. She'd grown up poor and experienced tough times being bullied as a child. Annie knew that her critics just didn't understand her.

In 1901, however, a terrible train crash forced her to retire to a less taxing career. This was a bit of a shock. But now that she didn't have to worry about traveling or performing anymore, Annie decided to "perform" differently. She acted in a stage play written for her! She used her rifle, wits, and rope to outsmart outlaws and save the day.

Annie made her shooting an art. She focused on practicing every day, rather than focusing on winning—because while she might not have been able to win every single contest, every day that she practiced was definitely a win.

Annie Oakley lived a very exciting life.
Let's see how much you remember from her story!

1. How old was Annie when she won the shooting competition against Frank E. Butler?
   a. 18
   b. 17
   c. 15
2. How many women did Annie teach to shoot?
   d. 15,000+ women
   e. 40,000 women
   f. 2 women

3. What was Annie Oakley's real name?
    g. Annie Mosey
    h. Phoebe Oakley
    i. Phoebe Ann Mosey
4. What was the Wild West show Annie joined with William Cody?
    j. Boston Bill's Wild West Show
    k. Buffalo Bill's Wild West Show
    l. Baltimore Bill's Wild West Show
5. What accident forced Annie to relax more in life?
    m. Train accident
    n. Car accident
    o. Bike accident

Answers (1. C - 2. A - 3. C - 4. B - 5. A)

5
RACHEL CARSON

Marine Conservationist | Environmentalist
Wonder Warrior of the Seas
May 27, 1907 - April 14, 1964
Springdale, Pennsylvania

"The more clearly we focus our attention on the wonders and realities of the universe about us, the less taste we shall have for destruction."

C rash!

The boat rocked and rolled, and another wave smashed into the hull's side. Rachel Carson and the other students were out on a study ship. They were doing a practical exercise.

Her grinning teacher was holding a small beaker. "This is why we've come," he said, as sea spray covered him from head to toe.

Before Rachel could see what her teacher was holding, another big wave crashed into their boat.

Splaaaash!

Sputtering water, Rachel tried to get up. She couldn't understand the point of this class. The teacher was the only one able to stand in the howling wind, anyway! And to make matters worse, he was laughing. "You'll get your sea legs soon!" he called.

"Why did we come out in a storm?" she asked, rising and falling back down again.

"Because why not!" her teacher called back. He gave her a hand to help her get up.

"Because it's crazy!" Rachel said. What was really crazy was that she'd left her safe writing degree for this!

Her teacher grinned and shook his head. "We didn't come out for this." He threw the beaker of water overboard. "We came out for the plankton!" He pointed behind her.

Rachel turned and her eyes went wide. The ocean was glowing—even with the storm raging. Waves rose and fell, and still the glowing blue light shone. It was magical. But even more so, it was beautiful. Suddenly, Rachel was glad she'd left her writing degree for this.

New ideas can feel scary when we don't understand what's happening—much like how Rachel felt on the boat in the storm. But if you ask for help and persevere, you can also see the beauty! Have you ever felt doubtful or unsure in your life while learning?

Rachel loved the ocean her whole life. But, as a kid, she'd originally wanted to be a writer, telling stories about the sea and its creatures. Her dreams hadn't involved science at all! That was, until something cool happened....

In university, Rachel took a biology class that changed everything. She was already in love with the ocean, but, after her biology class, she was in love with the science of the ocean.

The watery world became one big puzzle, and Rachel was determined to solve it. She learned all sorts of amazing things. Soon, this delightful, scary, magnificent, strange world made sense. And the best part? She didn't need to make anything up! The ocean was more fascinating than she could imagine. Rachel couldn't wait to share her ideas with people.

This class convinced Rachel to become a scientist who worked with the ocean—a marine biologist. It was so interesting that she didn't want to stop. She studied at Chatham University, then Johns Hopkins University, always discovering more and more about the hidden world of the sea. All the while, she continued sharing what she learned through her writing.

Once her studies were done, she got a temporary job with the US Bureau of Fisheries, writing scripts for the radio and promoting the ocean and its life. Her passion and knowledge, in addition to her writing skills, impressed her supervisor immensely. After she was done, they helped her take an entrance exam to get a proper job, and Rachel outscored everyone! She became the second woman to be hired by the State Department, and began her career as a junior aquatic biologist.

But, that's not all... Once she began working for the Bureau of Fisheries, Rachel wanted to tell even more people about the ocean, so she began writing more than ever. She didn't need to tell stories about mermaids, pirates, treasure, or anything fantastical—the ocean was already magical! It was filled with incredible fish and beautiful coral reefs, glowing plankton and magnificent whales—there just wasn't anyone telling the public!

So Rachel wrote about everything under the water, and also talked about the important role the ocean played on planet Earth. She told people how they could help, and also why they should help.

Being a girl scientist wasn't always easy. Lots of men didn't believe that girls were smart enough, and they didn't like that Rachel wanted to change the world. While their words often hurt Rachel, the ideas she was talking about were important. So she decided to be fearless and continued spreading her ideas! And the biggest one was just around the corner....

The release of *Silent Spring* in 1962 became her biggest splash yet. Rachel's book warned people about how chemicals being used on land were harming the ocean. This made people want to take action. The American government liked her thinking, and soon formed the US Environmental Protection Agency.

However, people from before who didn't like Rachel being a female scientist still had problems. They said hurtful things about her. Fortunately, Rachel ignored them.

Deep down, she knew that what she was doing was important. And with *Silent Spring*, there were a lot of other people who agreed with her!

Rachel spent her life exploring below the waves. To get a sense of her life, let's make an Ocean Sensory Bottle!

What you'll need for this project:

- An empty plastic bottle
- Clear hair gel
- Aqua glitter
- Mini ocean animals that fit through your bottle opening (note that these are little toys you can find at most toy shops.)
- Blue and green food coloring
- Bowl for mixing
- Funnel
- Water

Let's visit the ocean!

1. The size of your bottle will determine how much water and gel you use, but for a slow-moving bottle, you'll be making a 6-to-1 ratio of water to gel. For a quicker-moving bottle, add less hair gel.

2. Add a drop of blue food dye to your water-and-gel mixture and mix well.

3. Add as much glitter to your mixture as you want. Then mix again.

4. Place the funnel into your bottle and pour in the mixture. Take out the funnel.

5. Add the mini ocean animals.

6. Twist the cap onto your bottle and give the whole thing a shake! Look at all the ocean life floating around in the bottle. What does it make you think or feel?

SPARK HER CREATIVITY & CONFIDENCE.
GET YOUR <u>FREE</u> BONUSES NOW!

BONUS #1: Affirmations Coloring Book
Color Her World With Positivity & Empowering Words

BONUS #2: Dream Big & Shine Bright Journal
A Guided Journal for Positivity, Dreams & Self-Discovery

BONUS #3: Affirmation Cards for Amazing Girls
Beautiful Cards to Recite Daily & Brighten Her Day

BONUS #4: Inspirational Quote Cards for Amazing Girls
Quotes from the Women in this Book!

Scan with your phone's camera
OR go to: https://bit.ly/3AMeZJ8

6
OPRAH WINFREY

Talk Show Host | Philanthropist
Enlightened Woman of Spirit
January 29 , 1954 – Present
Kosciusko, Mississippi

*"When you undervalue what you do, the world
will undervalue who you are."*

"**I** heard you," her boss cut in. "And I'll ask again: Why?"

Oprah frowned. "Because we work the same job. We interview the same people. We do the same things. I believe I've earned the right."

"But *why* do *you* need to earn the same as him?"

Oprah pursed her lips. Her boss was making her feel silly. The way he spoke to her hurt her feelings. All her visualizations that morning had been of her succeeding. She had seen herself laughing and having fun— not *justifying* being paid the same as a boy.

"I'm entitled to fair pay," Oprah said finally. "We do the same work. I work hard. I think—I know—I'm entitled to the same pay."

Oprah's boss smirked. "Well, it's good that you think so."

Oprah grunted and shook her head. Her boss wanted what was best for himself and the studio. She wasn't even on their mind.

A spiritual power of her ancestors rose in Oprah—a belief she found empowering. She sat straighter in her chair and met her boss eye to eye. If she wasn't paid fairly here, she wouldn't stay.

Oprah smiled. "Thanks for your time." She rose and left. "I'm done."

"Wait, hold on," her boss said, sitting forward quickly as understanding dawned on his face. "What do you mean you're done?"

Oprah turned and smiled, "I mean, I quit."

Have you ever had to dig down into your stomach and find the strength to stand up for your beliefs? Or what about making a hard decision— have you had to make one of those?

At that moment, Oprah was listening to her gut instinct. It was scary, but it was what she had to do to grow.

She was being fearless when she left that job to chase her future. Oprah didn't know what to do next, but she knew who she was—which was more important. The dreams she'd had of success reminded her she had to work with people who believed in her. There were plenty of broadcasters who knew who she was and who would jump at the chance to work with her.

While her success didn't happen overnight, the woman she became in that moment followed her from state broadcasting to global super-stardom. Oprah decided she wouldn't allow others to control the value she saw in herself—not anymore.

Not ever.

But, that's not all... While we know Oprah as a megastar now, in the 1980s, her new show was a big risk for everyone. Soon, the world fell in love with this funny, smart, kind woman who connected with people truthfully. Oprah made everyone feel safe. More than that, she made them feel proud to be who they were. For over 20 years, Oprah was the queen of the talk shows. She changed how talk shows were viewed. Helping other talk show hosts with their shows was her way of giving back. Oprah just wanted to help empower people, which is why she got the audience involved with her shows. Their participation was fun. It was exciting. And, for the biggest surprise, she gave her audience gifts, too (gifts that were sometimes life-changing!).

Even if it was called a talk show, Oprah's superpower was that she was a great listener. Sometimes, the best way to help people is to listen to their problems. Of course, Oprah would also make them laugh and feel better about themselves.

This was because Oprah knew what it was like to feel sad. She understood what it was like to not feel proud of herself. Life hadn't always been easy for her. When she was young, her parents divorced and she lived with her mother. Times were tough, and she was bursting with emotions she didn't fully understand. They were so poor she once had to wear a potato sack!

Eventually, Oprah was placed in her father's care, and with him she learned responsibility. She learned how important education was, and that it was good to help others, too (even if a bit of hard work was involved). She learned a lot, and it was the tough times that ended up helping make her successful.

The Queen of Talk Shows had a big impact outside of TV, too. Oprah loved books and reading. She also loved recommending books to her fans, and any time Oprah recommended a book on her show, fans would flock to buy it. This became known as the "Oprah Effect." From the tens of millions of viewers that tuned in each week to watch her show to the millions of books she helped sell through her book club, her goal of helping people was changing lives every day.

Today, Oprah still talks to people who inspire her, and their interviews get broadcast on her own network. She still has her book club, and she even has a magazine! But, most importantly, she still teaches people to believe in themselves, and that they should feel loved for who they are.

Oprah has always told her fans that they should believe in themselves. Do you believe in yourself? Here are five affirmations (helpful sayings) to keep you feeling good.

1. "I am loved and appreciated."
2. "I am brave and strong."
3. "I am kind and honest."
4. "I am proud of who I am."
5. "I am full of creativity and imagination."

7
ANNA MAY WONG

Film Star ǀ Silver Screen Trailblazer ǀ Dramatic Queen

January 3, 1905 – February 3, 1961

Los Angeles, California

*"I was always made to feel I was half Chinese
and half American, but I am not half anything,
I am all one."*

Her seat squeaked as Anna May Wong tried to shuffle deeper into it.

Dust specks floating in the air shone in the projector light. Only a few people sat in the cinema with Anna. She was meant to be at school, but instead she was getting excited for the next scene.

Nervous joy was building in her. She could barely keep still. The actors may as well have not been there. She only cared for what was behind them in the background: *her neighborhood.*

The theater door opened and the attendant looked in. Anna turned out of habit.

"Hey!" he shouted.

Anna jumped from her chair and ran! Adrenaline flooded through her body. The attendant chased after her and yelled to stop, but Anna jumped onto the bench, sprang across two aisles, and sprinted for the opposite theater door!

"Stop sneaking into the theater, kid!" the attendant called.

Anna laughed, too giddy to care.

The reason she snuck into the cinema was because she wanted to be an actress. She wanted to see actors that looked like her on the screen. With enough self-belief, she believed she could do it, too!

Anna burst into the warm Los Angeles sunlight, then stopped cold at what she saw.

Frustration brewed in her belly. There was a poster on the wall for a new film with actors pretending to be Asian-American. They were wearing makeup called "yellow face."

The doors swung open and the attendant arrived. "You can't keep sneaking in, Anna. You're meant to be in school."

"But this is my school," Anna said. "I'm going to be an actress. I'm gonna be on the screen one day, and then there'll be no more of that *yellow face!*" she said, pointing at the poster.

Are there any stories you'd like to act out? Acting is like playing pretend, except you're following a story. What about pretending to be one of your favorite characters? Do you go on adventures?

Anna May Wong never gave up on her dream to act, or the belief that all people should be able to act. It was this perseverance that helped her be successful. It wasn't easy, though. Some days, Anna hung around film sets to be an extra, or haunted the locations where they would film movies in real life. She also talked to people working in film. And after a few years, she started landing roles.

But Anna wasn't just happy to be in the movies. She was determined to show the world how awesome Asian people were. She wanted to portray herself on screen the way she deserved to be seen. While she was now an actor, Anna was sad that Hollywood enforced silly rules that always made Asian people the villains or sidekicks—or, in her case, a murderer. She wanted empowering roles to inspire girls, yet she wasn't even allowed to fall in love on screen!

As a trailblazer, Anna faced a lot of pressure. Luckily, she was fearless! Despite people saying horrible things about her race and the fact that she was a girl, she kept going. She proved them wrong with her acting skills.

But, that's not all... The list of awesome things Anna May Wong did in her acting career is far more than what most achieve in a lifetime! Not only was she the first Chinese-American film star, she was also the first to gain worldwide fame. She acted in silent films, one of the first color films, and the first "talkies" (before 1927, all films were silent!). She achieved all of this, despite the racism that was in Hollywood!

Even with all this success, it was still difficult for Anna to be an actor in Hollywood because of her ethnicity. Obstacles were constantly thrown in her face. Some directors didn't want Asians acting, so they would cast white people to play the roles and then put makeup on them. If Anna did win a role, it was often a negative one. She would be a villain, or have to act as a really bad stereotype of her culture. It felt demeaning.

Anna vowed to not accept these roles. She decided she wouldn't give up on being true to herself. She would practice really hard and be so good they couldn't ignore her. She might not get lead roles, but at least she would act in roles she was proud of.

Anna's acting friends loved working with her, and their opinions helped her get work, as well.

As a trailblazer, Anna realized how important TV would soon become. Because she was used to acting in movies, on stage, and on the radio, television was just another area for her to try. So she began acting on TV, and that was where she truly found acceptance. This shift allowed her to become the first Chinese-American woman to lead a television show!

Anna's fearlessness kept her going. Despite the challenges, she loved what she did. Her self-belief took her from being a child watching the screen to a woman *on* the screen.

And on the days when she didn't necessarily believe she could do it, she acted like she did—which is an important skill, too!

Have you tried acting? Here are some fun exercises to try!

These exercises can be done for 5-10 minutes, or as long as you want to have fun! Acting is all about being comfortable in your body.

1. **Seashore:** Pretend you're a piece of seaweed in the water. With the waves washing over you, how do you sway? Are they calm or stormy waves? Does the pull of the ocean tip you over? Or perhaps you are a seashell being washed up on the shore. What about a crab?
2. **Mirror, Mirror:** Stand facing a friend and decide who will go first. The first person makes a funny face, gesture, or dance, then the other person has to copy it. For an extra challenge, try not to laugh!
3. **Freeze Dance with Feelings:** Play upbeat music and begin dancing around. When the music stops, the person controlling the music calls out an emotion (happy, angry, sad, scared, etc). Try your best to act it out!

8
SALLY RIDE

Astronaut | **Advocate for STEM** | **Goddess of Space**

May 26, 1951 – July 23, 2012

Los Angeles, California

"The stars don't look bigger,
but they do look brighter."

It takes eight and a half minutes to go from 0 to 175,000 miles an hour strapped to a rocket.

But more importantly, it took eight and a half minutes for Sally Ride to become the first American woman in space!

Her hands were shaking and her body was full of nervous excitement. Thunder was rumbling around the ship.

Whoooooooooooooosh! *Flump*! BOOOOM!!

The fuel engines detached. Then, the shuttle took on a feeling of weightlessness that Sally couldn't describe. All she knew was that the eight and a half minutes were up.

"It looks just like a map, doesn't it?" her crewmate said.

"It does," she muttered in awe.

Earth was below them, and the pictures hadn't done it justice.

Clouds formed and dispersed. Seas swelled and crashed. Mountains rose in the same way as the waves, then ebbed and fell to rolling hills and desert. Cities winked like stars.

The globe spun and stood still at the same time. If Sally blinked, she'd miss it all.

All those years studying—the late nights and long classes—were suddenly gone. All that mattered now was this moment.

Sally was in space.

She'd been picked to fly on the *Challenger* Space Shuttle because she was smart, talented, a whiz with her science and math, and, most importantly, an inspiring girl!

Do you ever look up at the stars and wonder what it's like to be in space? What is your favorite thing about space and the universe? Is there anything you'd like to know more of?

5... 4... 3... 2... 1... Blast off!

On the 18th of June, 1983, Sally rocketed into space. She became the first American woman, youngest American astronaut, and first LGBT astronaut to fly into space!

Sally spent six days in orbit with the crew. She used the shuttle robot arm—which is like a giant claw—to pick things up and put them down. They used this arm to do experiments and fix the shuttle. They also used it to take a photograph of the space shuttle itself!

The mission was a blast, except for one issue. The only problem Sally and her crewmates had was they had to land the shuttle somewhere unexpected because of bad weather. But even with this hiccup, Sally and her crewmates were instant celebrities.

But, that's not all... Sally's journey into space began long before 1983! Ever since she was a kid, she'd loved science. In fact, Sally had decided she would be an astrophysicist when she was just 17!

Sally also loved playing tennis and thinking about philosophy. Whether she was talking about Shakespeare's plays with her friends or winning in straight sets on the tennis court, she excelled at everything she did.

Sally wasn't always sure that she wanted to be a scientist, though. She was super good at both tennis and science. Both were really important to her, but a career in tennis would require her to practice even more than she currently was…so Sally decided to pursue the coolest frontier of them all—space!

This meant doing a lot of hard work. In the 1970s, Sally faced a lot of hurdles simply because she was a girl. She had to work very hard to prove her abilities to the male scientists. But this didn't stop her.

Once she was at NASA, she began making a name for herself. She worked with the legends and geniuses of space exploration, helped run missions from Mission Control as a capsule communicator, and eventually blasted off into space itself. She aimed for the stars and flew straight towards them!

Sally visited space a second time with NASA, but after a shuttle exploded on launch in 1986, she thought it was time for a change. She helped with the investigation to understand what had happened to the shuttle and her friends. Then, when it was finished, she decided that she wanted to teach others how to reach for the stars.

Sally retired from being an astronaut to become an awesome professor. When she wasn't teaching, she wrote books for children about science. She continued playing tennis, too, and lived out the rest of her life with her partner, Tam O'Shaughnessy.

Sally's goal was to make learning fun and fascinating. Science didn't have to be hard. She wanted it to be accessible for everyone. Because of her hard work, science has become a way for lots of kids to reach for the stars…even if they're still on planet Earth!

The best way to understand science is to see it! To understand the explosive power that sent Sally into space, let's make a water bottle rocket!

The chemical reaction between vinegar and sodium bicarbonate (baking soda) is explosive!

NOTE: *Do this activity outside (and with an adult)!*

What do you need?

- An empty soda bottle
- 3 tbsp of baking soda (sodium bicarbonate)
- 2 cups vinegar
- Paper towel
- A cork (or something to stuff the end of your bottle with that can shoot out)
- A launchpad for your rocket (something that holds your bottle upside down and off the ground)
- Adult supervision

Now, let's make this rocket fly!

1. After decorating your rocket, place vinegar in the bottle.
2. Cut your paper towel into a four-inch square.
3. Place a heaping tablespoon of baking soda into the paper towel. Fold up the paper towel with the baking soda at the center and keep folding until you can fit into the opening of your bottle.
4. Push the baking soda paper towel into your bottle.
5. Put in the cork so it's nice and snug.
6. Flip it over and place the rocket on the launchpad!
7. Get ready for lift off!

9
BILLIE JEAN KING

Tennis Legend | Gender Equality in Sports Activist | Ace of a Woman

November 22, 1943 – Present

Long Beach, California

"Create your legacy, and pass the baton!"

Click! Flash!

The cameras flashed as Billie Jean King smashed the tennis ball with her deadly forehand. The ball spun back over the net, but her opponent made it just in time and whacked the ball back!

Billie Jean ran as fast as she could for it. She didn't think she'd make it, but then she swung her racket with all her strength. She aimed away from her opponent and the ball shot down the line for the win!

"Game. Set. Match!"

Billie Jean had just won the US Open!

She fell to her knees with joy. Her body flooded with adrenaline, even though she was exhausted. She wiped the sweat and tears of joy from her eyes and stood up, then smiled and waved at the crowd.

Billie Jean went to the net and congratulated her opponent, then got a drink. It was thirsty work being a tennis legend!

But all that work and dedication was paying off for Billie Jean! She was happy...until she was given her winnings. Then she was angry.

A sour lump formed in her stomach. It grew and grew until she was looking at all the journalists in front of her and not wanting to be there. She almost felt like she didn't want to play tennis anymore! But she'd figured out what the problem was, and how she'd fix it.

It was an ace no one would expect.

"Missus King? Missus King?"

Billie Jean could still feel the soft fur of the tennis ball in her palms and the worn leather grip of the racket in her fingertips. Her hands tingled and her legs were wobbly.

"Will you be defending your title next year?" someone asked.

Billie Jean looked down at her hands. She wanted to be valued for what she was worth. "I don't think we'll be coming back," she said.

Silence filled the room.

"I haven't spoken to the other women yet, but I don't think we'll be coming back unless we get equal prize money."

The silence turned to chaos. Journalists yelled questions over each other. The US Open competition manager came out in a hurry, but Billie Jean was already walking away from the microphone and leaving the room.

Billie Jean was a superstar tennis player, but she didn't like how she and the other girls were treated. Have you ever listened to your gut and spoken up? Do you feel that sometimes things don't seem right?

From that one small sentence, the whole world of women's tennis changed!

Billie Jean King was already a legendary tennis player by 1972. She was the best of the best. She had reached the number one spot years earlier in 1966, and all of her hard work and efforts had been recognized.

But there was a problem. Girls weren't getting paid as much as boys— even if they were practicing just as much (or more!). This was a problem Billie Jean constantly faced. All women players back then were underappreciated. They were looked down upon. Some people even said they were less skilled! As the player at the top of her field, Billie Jean did something about it and fought back.

That legendary interview became a moment in history that changed the fortunes for all women in all sports. Billie Jean demanded that they be treated fairly—and it worked!

While it wasn't easy, Billie Jean spent the next year talking with companies that also wanted to help women athletes get equal pay. She spent a lot of time talking with sponsors, and in the process created a special league just for women. By 1973, Billie Jean and all the women not only played again in the US Open, but they were also paid as much as the men! (Billie Jean also became the first woman to earn over $100,000 in prize money for winning a tennis competition!)

But, that's not all... Billie Jean King, or BJK, as her nickname became, is not only one of the best female tennis players ever, she's also one of the best tennis players *period*.

Billie Jean's greatest talent with the racket was that she could play both singles and doubles really well. Playing with another person means you have to be a good team player, and Billie Jean was one of the best. No matter the style of play, she was a force to be reckoned with.

1973 was a big year, because women earned equal prize money at the US Open. But it was also big for another reason. A famous male tennis player called Bobby Riggs thought girls weren't as good as boys. He spent a lot of time telling everyone this. He also began challenging women tennis players, and created a "Battle of the Sexes" match. At first, Billie Jean didn't want to play him, but when he became too annoying, she decided to teach him a lesson.

The game became a huge deal! It was months in the making. In the end, over 90 million people worldwide watched Billie Jean King beat Bobby

Riggs in front of more than 30,000 live spectators. What's more, Billie Jean won in straight sets and was awarded $100,000 dollars for her win!

Billie Jean's performance was a victory for girls everywhere. She showed everyone that girls were just as capable as boys. A new era of women's tennis had begun!

Billie Jean's fearlessness on the court was also how she fought for equal rights and pay off the court. Promoting the first professional women's tennis tour was tough, but with her win over Bobby Riggs on TV, she proved how good she and the other players were. They were just as exciting to watch as the men.

In a cool twist, her game with Bobby triggered a whole new wave of feminism. It created a ripple effect that helped many more women around the world, not just those playing tennis. Most importantly, Billie Jean King's efforts laid the foundation for many more great tennis player's to follow!

Have you tried playing tennis? In the spirit of Billie Jean's awesome tennis fun, here are three fun tennis activities to try!

These activities can be played for between 5-30 minutes—or, if you're having fun, play as long as you want!

1. **Balloon Tennis**: If you're new to playing tennis, then balloon tennis could be a great way for you to learn (it can also be a lot of fun!). Using your racket, hit a balloon back and forth with a partner or group. You can also hit it back and forth over a net.

2. **Catch Tennis**: For this activity, we're putting down the rackets. This game is all about developing your hand-eye connection. You'll play tennis just like normal, but you can catch and throw the ball back to your partner.

3. **Glow-in-the-Dark Tennis**: This one is for kids who are confident with their skills and like playing in the dark! You can buy glow-in-the-dark tennis balls, and with a few glowsticks for kids to wear on necklaces, you can have fun on a court with little to no lighting!

10
GRACE HOPPER

**US Navy Rear Admiral | Pioneer Computer
Programmer | Coder Extraordinaire**
December 9, 1906 - January 1, 1992
New York, New York

*"The most dangerous phrase in the language
is 'We've always done it this way.'"*

G race Hopper stopped. *That couldn't be it?*
She was standing in the hot and sweaty UNIVAC computer room, hands on hips, feeling very frustrated. The command hadn't worked—again!

But now she was looking at the problem, and it was so simple she felt silly.

She untangled the wires leading to the command keyboard and saw that they were plugged into the wrong sockets.

Grace laughed and corrected her mistake. She flicked the power button, and the computer burst to life again. Gauges lit up and flashed with electricity, the generator hummed, and the printer beeped that it was ready. Grace returned to the desk for one last try. Would it work now?

Could word prompts really control this enormous computer with simple English?

Grace typed a simple command of "0" on the keyboard and hit enter.

The computer whirred and switches switched. The tape relays activated and the computer began retrieving data. The printer made a grinding noise and began printing out the input inventory! Grace felt giddy with joy.

She typed "17" for the computer to stop.

Her heart was racing. The FLOW-MATIC coding language was working perfectly with the new language they'd invented. Now for the big test.

She gulped, then typed "Identification Division" and hit enter. The computer processed the command and dropped to a new line. It was waiting for her next command. It was working!

Grace's idea had come to life. She cried out with joy. She'd proved them all wrong! With this new idea, computers were going to change the world.

Grace's math skills were just one of the many ways she solved problems with computing. Another was asking simple questions (solving problems in STEM subjects often involves simple questions). Asking why something is happening is often a great way to find your answer!

While Grace Hopper was originally a math whiz, she soon became a computer whiz, too, thanks to her probing questions and ability to make hard concepts easy to understand.

But before Grace had the opportunity to use computers, she had to get into the Navy...and they didn't want her!

When America entered World War II, Grace wanted to help by joining the Navy. Unfortunately, she had lots of problems trying to enlist, as they said she was too old and underweight. But Grace didn't want to do physical battle—she wanted to help with her greatest asset, her mind. Luckily for us, a recruiter recognized how helpful she could be working with computers, and Grace was eventually signed up.

There was just one problem: Grace didn't know anything about computers! However, she was a math whiz, which is why the recruiter had liked her! Back then, computers ran on handwritten "programming cards," and these cards were made up of mathematical equations and symbols, binary code, and eventually words. Being able to write high-level math equations meant Grace could program the computer at its highest capabilities.

Filled with nervous excitement, Grace started her adventure. She was sent to Harvard to work on a super gigantic computer called the Mark I. However, her boss was frustrated about the fact that he'd been given a girl to help with his work, so he decided to give Grace the boring job of writing a computer manual (the first ever). The joke was on him, because Grace loved this! Her problem of knowing nothing about computers now turned into a great opportunity to learn, and her manual turned out to be so good that her boss completely changed his view on women and computers. He made Grace his top programmer.

The whole time Grace was studying how the computer physically worked, she also wondered how she could make things easier. How could computers be programmed more easily?

Grace loved all of it. She understood the computer better than most, so when it came to programming, she had lots of ideas about how to do it better. She was hooked!

Grace loved computers so much that, even after World War II, she didn't want to stop working with them. She decided to stay in the Navy and make computers her career. She bravely explored the wild frontier of computers, even though most men didn't think girls should be part of it.

Sexism wasn't the only challenge she faced. What worked one day soon changed and didn't work the next. Programs and ideas were evolving quickly. Again, Grace wondered if there was an easier way. Solving this problem would become her lifelong achievement.

But, that's not all... Grace's thinking and ideas truly changed computers. She saw what computers were capable of before others saw it. It was all about problem solving, and the problem Grace had been dealing with would soon be solved with a simple idea.

When she first started telling people her idea, they told her it was impossible. Men all throughout the computer world told her the idea was bad and that she should forget it. But Grace knew they were wrong.

What was the idea?

By the 1950s, computers had come a long way thanks to Grace and lots of other smart people. But no one had figured out how to make using the computer easier. That was, until Grace came up with a program to translate English words into computer code. Think of it like a modern day translator. Grace put in an English word prompt, and out came the code the computer could understand.

This development was huge. It changed how computers were used and helped turn them into what we know today. Grace's computer language, COBOL, is still used today, and is a mainstay at big companies such as IBM!

Grace received many honors in her lifetime. From semi-inventing the term "debugging" by finding a real (dead) moth in their code cards to receiving the Presidential Medal of Freedom because of her invention of COBOL, whatever Grace put her hands on, she managed to turn it into a success.

Her achievements live on through the biggest female and non-binary tech conference in the world, called the Grace Hopper Convention. It celebrates women in STEM and encourages all girls to dream big, dream tech, and dream of answers not yet found.

Grace Hopper achieved a lot in her life.
Here are five fun facts!

1. Grace was so curious as a child that she took apart seven alarm clocks to see how they worked.
2. Grace was the oldest active-duty officer in the Navy's history!
3. Besides inventing the COBOL computer language, Grace also "spoke" many other computer languages.
4. Her nickname was Amazing Grace.
5. In 2016, Grace was awarded the Presidential Medal of Freedom!

11
ELEANOR ROOSEVELT

First Lady of United States | Human Rights Activist
Grandmother to a Nation

October 11, 1884 – November 7, 1962

New York, New York

"You must do the thing you think you cannot do!"

"**R**ight, ladies, it's just us. Have you got any questions before I begin?"

Every hand shot up.

All the reporters sitting in front of Eleanor Roosevelt were women. She was holding the first all-female presidential press conference for female reporters, on behalf of her husband, Franklin.

Eleanor chuckled. "To guess what these first questions are—yes, the president knows we're having an all-female press conference. He's very happy for us." A few of the hands went down, and all the women were smiling. "Any other questions?"

All the hands shot back up.

"You there."

A woman in a brown dress and green jacket spoke in a burst of excitement. She barely took a breath. "This is all so exciting. What other rules will you be breaking as the First Lady?" She sat down, then stood back up. "Thank you, Madam First Lady." She sat down again.

Everyone laughed, but Eleanor the most. She, too, was excited to be creating change.

"Firstly, I'm not breaking any rules. We're correcting rules that should have always been more inclusive. As for the rest of what I intend to do as First Lady—" Eleanor put on a serious face. "I refuse to sit by and watch America from the sidelines."

Thunderous applause filled the room.

"I have always believed in helping people. It is what makes me feel alive. I cannot sit here while America fights this Great Depression. I cannot sit here and entertain others while many Americans are unemployed. I cannot sit here and pretend to be happy, while our great nation fights through this sad time. So I won't! In the next days, months, and years, you will not find me here, but there. Everywhere. America is my White House. Not this building. I intend on acting like a First Lady you've never seen!"

The applause became louder.

Eleanor didn't need to tell them it wouldn't be easy. The US was a big country with many different opinions. But it was her duty as First Lady to try and listen to as many people as possible.

From listening to people's problems to writing about her own, Eleanor always found a way to help. One of the best ways she believed we could help was through volunteering. Have you ever thought of volunteering your time to help people or solve a problem in your neighborhood?

If empathy was a superpower, then Eleanor Roosevelt was a superhero!

When Eleanor was a teenager at Allenswood Boarding School in England, she first saw who her future self could be. Having lost both parents by the age of 10, Eleanor had been brought up by her grandmother. She was a strict lady who hadn't given Eleanor any self-confidence. But attending Allenswood introduced the young girl to a world where she was treated like an adult—even as a teenager! They talked about difficult topics and were encouraged to care for and help others. Eleanor even learned to speak French! Her schooling was nothing like her experiences in America. For Eleanor, boarding school was empowering. She became a new person.

So that's what she set about doing when she came back to America—she would empower anyone and everyone! She would listen and find a way to help others, just as she had been helped.

Eleanor's life of helping others soon introduced her to her future husband, a man called Franklin D. Roosevelt...and what a meeting that was! Franklin also enjoyed helping people, but on a bigger level. Soon, he would be sworn in as President of the United States, and Eleanor would become the First Lady.

It was a hard time to be president, as America had entered the Great Depression. But just because she was now the First Lady, Eleanor didn't believe she should sit around and welcome guests for tea. One of the first things Eleanor said when Franklin became president was that she would not be like the First Ladies who came before her.

Most First Ladies retired to life within the White House. They accepted guests and entertained, stopped advocating for causes they believed in, and made sure not to step into their husbands' limelight. But Eleanor didn't believe she would outshine her husband—she believed she would only support him! So, along with entertaining guests at the White House, she also continued her support of human rights, women's suffrage, and social work. She believed everything she did would help her husband.

Of course, Eleanor was already helping her husband in another way. Most people didn't realize that Franklin had been paralyzed from the waist down since 1921 because of polio. Eleanor had been speaking and traveling on his behalf since before he became president! No one had had any issues with her then, so why stop now?

Eleanor drove all over the country, meeting folks left, right, and center. Some years, she drove over 40,000 miles! She did this because she cared for the people of America. She wanted to know their problems and what was affecting them, so she could tell Franklin. As president, he could make decisions to help everyone.

They were so popular that Franklin was voted in as president four times in a row! The people of America felt heard.

But, that's not all... After World War II, Eleanor believed it was now more important than ever that people's rights were defended. Too much sadness had come from World War II, as well as America's own history. So Eleanor set off for the United Nations. In fact, she was appointed by the next president, Harry S. Truman! And it was through talking with other countries that she would have her largest impact.

After years of writing, in 1948, Eleanor presented the Universal Declaration of Human Rights. It was a big deal. She even received a standing ovation. The document was a guide on how to treat people. Plus, it was made with the help of all the countries in the United Nations, and they all wanted to uphold its ideals.

Protecting people throughout the world was how Eleanor wanted to make an impact, but just because the document existed, that didn't mean it was enforced...or that everyone liked what she was doing.

Eleanor had dedicated her life to helping people feel heard, seen, and accepted, but during the early and mid-1900s in America, human rights causes were a lot of trouble for a lot of people. She supported African-Americans and the Civil Rights cause, as well as equality for women in the workplace, but there were lots of people who didn't like her ideas. They thought that she shouldn't have an opinion on anything because she was a girl!

Because of her years as First Lady and talking to people and helping, Eleanor knew that getting this reaction meant she was doing the right thing. Change is often like that. It ruffles feathers!

Eleanor Roosevelt was a fearless pioneer in many ways. She changed the way all First Ladies acted during the presidency, and was also a fearless human rights supporter. She wanted the people of America to understand that we were all part of something bigger, and that we are deserving of hope and peace.

Eleanor was practically a superhero! Here are five fun facts about her to help you better understand what she accomplished.

1. Eleanor overcame being a shy girl, and eventually came to love public speaking.
2. Eleanor believed the best way to "meet the people" was to drive her car around the US. Some years, she drove over 40,000 miles!!!
3. Eleanor loved wearing bright red sunglasses—which many people considered to be too flamboyant at the time.
4. Eleanor Roosevelt was bilingual and could speak French fluently.
5. Eleanor wrote a newspaper column called My Day for almost 30 years!

12
RITA MORENO

**Singer and Dancer | Only Latinx Person to Reach
EGOT Status | Women of Dance**

December 11, 1931 – Present

Humacao, Puerto Rico

*"Bigger than life is not a problem for me.
I am bigger than life."*

"**A**nd the Oscar for Best Supporting Actress goes to...."

The room held its breath. Rita Moreno held hers, too. She was nervous and her stomach felt like it was full of worms! She *knew* it wasn't going to be her, but in the deepest corner of her heart, she wished it would be.

All the other actresses were so good! Rita felt she had nothing on Judy Garland, not to mention Fay Bainter, Lotte Lenay, and Une Merkel! She shook in her seat just thinking about it all. She'd been practicing her losing face all morning.

Rock Hudson looked up from the envelope in his hand and smiled at the crowd with his sparkling eyes. He looked around the crowd and slowly found his way towards Rita.

Then he smiled even wider. "Rita Moreno for *West Side Story.*"

Rita's eyes went wide. Her heart stopped. She couldn't believe it! She stood and smiled in a daze, hugged her friends and began making her way to the podium.

Don't run, she thought. Don't run at all, it's not dignified.

She made it to the stairs and began climbing. What would she say? Would she thank anyone? Or should she?

A resolve came over her. *She wouldn't thank anyone.* They hadn't given her this part because of a favor, they'd given it to her because she'd had the best audition!

"Well done," Rock said as Rita leaned in for a hug and accepted the award. Rita held it in her hands and stepped up to the podium.

If she wasn't going to thank anyone, what was she going to say? Her mind went blank.

"I can't believe it! Good Lord! I leave you with that." Rita smiled at the crowd and then left.

The acceptance soundtrack was still winding down, and it had to start back up! The ceremony had just experienced one of the shortest acceptance speeches ever.

Finally, someone like her—someone with a Latinx background—was being recognized for their skill!

Do you like musicals? Have you tried singing, acting, and dancing all together? Maybe you could find some musicals to watch with your parents or guardian, and play pretend after?

Rita Moreno's win at the Oscar was a huge deal.

She became the first Latinx woman to win an Oscar (one of the many awards she'd go on to win in her life). And the film itself became legendary! All the actors that were involved were great. Rita made lots of friends, and the film was very successful (in fact, it won lots of other awards, too!).

Although Rita's win was historic, it didn't change much for Latinx people in the film industry, or even the roles Rita was offered afterwards. This frustrated her and made her sad. So Rita returned to where she'd begun and what she loved most—musicals!

Rita loved singing and dancing more than anything. It was what made her happy. For almost 10 years, she stayed away from films and acted in roles in musicals that empowered and inspired her. She hoped her acting would inspire everyone else, too. She knew little girls looked up to her now, so she had to be the best role model she could be!

But, that's not all... Remember the Oscar that Rita won? Well, years later, she won an award called an Emmy...then one called a Grammy...and then one called a Tony. Finally, she even won one called a Peabody, plus three Golden Globes! These awards celebrate acting, dancing, and singing, and they're super difficult to win—especially all of them! Only a handful of performers have accomplished an EGOT, which is winning an Emmy, Grammy, Oscar, and Tony.

But Rita did it—plus she won a Peabody and a bunch of Golden Globes, too!

Rita Moreno was only the third person to achieve an EGOT, and the first Puerto Rican (and Latinx person) to do so. Throughout history, only 19 people have done it!

While it's easy to list these wins now, at the time, it took a lot of hard work. Rita didn't become famous overnight, and her success didn't come easily. She faced problems with racism and sexism, and had to fight for equality for women. Another issue she faced was that she'd been born in another country and came to America as a little girl. Some people didn't like this. But for Rita, it was just a part of the story that made her life inspiring! Her self-belief made her fearless.

She remained strong for all the other girls and women, so she could inspire them!

This is why she began singing and acting on kids' TV, too. It was her way of showing kids who she was and what they could become. From singing and dancing with *The Muppets* to being a regular on the children's show *The Electric Company*, Rita was teaching kids that "if they could see it, they could be it!"

Singing and dancing had always been a way for Rita to express herself, but it also feels good! If you ever need to feel happy or powerful, remember Rita and have some fun singing and dancing!

Rita loves singing so much that she's still doing it now. Have you tried singing?

1. Rita sang and danced on stage in musicals. See if you can attend a local musical with a parent or guardian!
2. Write a list of your favorite songs and print out the lyrics to learn them.
3. Try singing your favorite story! Simply pick a book and make up a melody to sing the book instead of speaking the words.

13
AUGUSTA SAVAGE

Sculptor I Civil Rights Activist I Sculptor of Change

February 29, 1892 – March 27, 1962

Green Cove Springs, Florida

"From the time I can first recall the rain falling on the red clay in Florida, I wanted to make things. When my brothers and sisters were making mud pies, I would be making ducks and chickens with the mud."

W hat if no one liked what she did?

Augusta Savage pushed that thought from her head, but it kept returning, so she focused on the small beetle crawling along the floor.

She was sitting outside the exam hall at the Cooper Union School of Art. She'd just taken an entrance exam and was waiting to hear if she'd be admitted to the school. Students walked by and openly stared—there weren't too many women around, let alone African-American women.

Augusta just hoped she'd done enough. Three hours was barely enough time to do anything, but she'd tried her best. That was all she could do.

The door opened and one of the judges appeared. "Miss Savage...."

She nodded and smiled, trying not to look as nervous as she felt. Augusta followed the judge back in and sat in front of the panel. Her sculpture sat by the wall.

"Miss Savage, it has been a unanimous decision from all of us here," said the judge in the middle.

Augusta's stomach plummeted. This was it. Here it came....

"We are blown away by your skill." All the judges smiled. "This sculpture is raw, chaotic, full of life and ambition. You said the idea was of a child reaching for the light, but what I see here is an artist reaching for her chance. Showing her abilities."

Augusta's jaw dropped.

"You are extremely gifted, and we'd like to accelerate your application. If you are willing, we will gladly place you in front of the current waiting list of 142 other people. You can start right away. What do you say?"

Augusta was flabbergasted. Had he said "gifted?" 142 other people? How did she beat...?

"Miss Savage?"

Augusta nodded her head. "I would love that very, very much. I would be honored."

"No," the judge said, smiling. "The honor will be ours."

What art class do you enjoy most at school? What have you made? If you were to teach it to others, would you teach clay and sculpture like Augusta, or a different medium?

From clay, Augusta Savage built history—talk about shaping a future!

1920s New York wasn't an easy place for an African-American artist and sculptor. While Augusta had experienced some recognition for her skills back in her home state of Florida, New York was a different place. She'd faced lots of racism and hardship in her life, but the Big Apple had doubled that. But while being rejected by art schools because of the color of her skin had made Augusta sad, it had also made her more determined.

This is what made her entrance into Cooper Union Art School so satisfying.

The school offered Augusta a full scholarship, and she would finish the course in three years instead of four. She soon finished her degree and began finding work.

The first job she got was a sculpture of W.E.B. Du Bois for the West 135th Library. It was amazing and people were impressed, but they wanted more! Soon, Augusta was working around the clock. She faced challenges with hard work and proved how skilled she was with her art.

Then, in 1923, Augusta got into a special, lesser-known summer program for great artists. It was in France at the Fontainebleau School of Fine Arts. Not only was Augusta super excited, she was also honored to finally get acknowledged by one of the biggest art programs in the world!

Unfortunately, for Augusta to officially get in, the committees in both France and America had to agree (as both were funding the trip). Everyone in France loved her work, but the American committee didn't like that she was African-American, so they took away her opportunity. It was really unfair!

Angry about the whole thing, Augusta wrote a letter to the *New York World* newspaper. A lot of people agreed that what was done to her was bad. It became big news worldwide, and other countries talked about it. But the American committee wouldn't change its mind. Augusta decided that she wouldn't give up on her artistic dreams, and took it as an opportunity to just keep trying and prove how good she was.

But, that's not all... Eventually, Augusta's hard work paid off in one of her greatest pieces—a sculpture for the 1939 World's Fair.

Augusta had lots of ideas, and knew she wanted to do something that would celebrate her life. Even more so, she wanted to do something that would celebrate *all* African-American lives.

Augusta was teaching at her own art school by this time, so she was super busy. Luckily, teaching others helped her refine her ideas, too. As she worked on her drawings and ideas, her vision slowly came to life. By 1939, she knew her sculpture would be special.

When the New York World's Fair began, people flocked to Augusta's statue. At 16 feet tall, her sculpture was enormous! And the effect was also big. People couldn't believe how beautiful it was and how skillfully it had been made. All the people wanted to do was keep looking at her wonderful statue.

Augusta had made a statue about the effect Black people had on music. She called it "Lift Every Voice and Sing." It was a statue of 12 African-American young people singing, with a young man playing music. But here's the twist: The people looked like they were part of a musical instrument called a harp, which is how the man was playing the music.

Augusta's statue was made into postcards and mini-statues, and lots of people took photos of it. It was a great success, and she was really happy! Unfortunately, when the fair ended, they destroyed it. This is because Augusta didn't have enough money to buy it from the World's Fair or have it cast in bronze. But while it only existed in pictures afterward, Augusta remained proud that she'd had the chance to make it.

Augusta believed in the importance of discovering who you were through your art. That's why she taught art, in addition to making her own. Not everyone can express their emotions like Augusta, but we can all learn to make art if we try hard enough!

Have you tried sculpting with clay?
Let's learn from Augusta and try!

For this activity, we'll be making an easy snake. Once you become more confident with sculpting, you can start making the shapes of any animal!

1. Cut off a good chunk of clay and roll it in your hands to make a ball.
2. Squish the ball flat and continue to roll it between your hands. When it looks like a cigar, place it on the counter and roll it under your hands until it looks like a snake's body.
3. You can either flatten one end to make the head or add more clay to have a bigger head.
4. Decorate it with beads or different colors of clay!

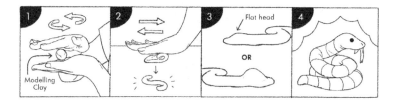

14
RUTH BADER GINSBERG

Associate Justice of the Supreme Court
Champion of Equality | Notorious RBG!

March 15, 1933 – September 18, 2020

Brooklyn, New York

*"Fight for the things that you care about. But do it
in a way that will lead others to join you."*

"And, so I ask, what would you have done?"

Ruth Bader Ginsberg looked each of the judges in the eye. The panel before her was big, but she was bigger. She no longer thought she might lose the case. She believed she could win it.

"I appeal to you not as judges, but as fathers' in your own rights. What would you have done?" Ruth held their stares. "My client here did what we all would do. Stephen had the joy of being a new father, and yet had to somehow find out how to be a widower. He of course went to Social Security for support. Survivor's benefits have helped many people before. However, they've all been women...."

Ruth paused.

"But here was a husband, a father, coming for help. And he was denied because he was a man. He was not deemed a survivor. We believe, as a society, that a man provides, but how could he raise his child and provide at the same time? Who would look after his child while he provided? And when could he grieve? When could he be a father?"

The judges were shifting uncomfortably in their seats. *She had them*.

"I don't think I need to argue that this is unconstitutional in our day and age. I don't need to argue whether it's right or wrong, either. You know," Ruth said, sitting down at the desk. "You know."

The judges retired to their chambers to decide their verdict. Ruth didn't have to wait long. They returned and agreed unanimously that it was unconstitutional that a person, *regardless of gender*, be denied survivor's benefits.

Ruth had won! It was another small brick in the wall of evidence she was building to show the world the unfair challenges women faced everyday—she just had to show the men what was happening to other men first, in order to make them think about women.

What do you think is fair? What do you think isn't? Ruth defended people regardless of who they were, as long as she thought they were being treated unfairly.

Ruth Bader Ginsburg was a super lawyer who fought for fairness and equality for girls and women. But being super had its drawbacks. As it turned out, Ruth was a super lawyer before boys and men were ready for her to be one.

Ruth graduated from college in 1959, and immediately wanted to change the world. But, because she was a woman, she had trouble finding work. Some men believed that women couldn't be lawyers, but Ruth persevered and found work teaching. From there, she started defending cases on the side.

In the 1970s, Ruth started revealing her true identity: *Super Judge!* She was now very experienced, but she was also even more frustrated at the inequality she saw all around her. Men continued to use her gender against her.

Then, Ruth had an idea. She would use their own arguments against them!

During the 1970s, she argued and won five important cases in the Supreme Court about inequality against men. When Ruth won, the judges had to admit that treating a person differently because of their gender was unfair. Ruth defended men who'd been treated unfairly because of their gender—then she showed how it was the same for women, too. The wins demonstrated Ruth's intelligence as a lawyer, but she was just getting started.

Talk about having an impact!

But, that's not all... Ruth didn't care what someone's gender, race, or culture was—she only wanted to listen and help solve the problem. In the 1970s, she started a law journal for women called the *Women's Rights Law Reporter.* As you might expect, it became very popular.

Slowly, the laws and times changed. And, slowly but surely, Ruth worked hard and moved up the ladder. She continued fighting for equal pay for girls, as well as equal opportunities for girls when it came to employment and benefits. Then, one day, she received a special phone call.

It was Bill Clinton. *The president.*

He wanted to create more equality in the Supreme Court system. A judge was retiring and he thought Ruth was the best fit to replace them.

It took a while for her to get nominated, but she was thrilled! Not only was Ruth the second woman to become a justice of the Supreme Court, she was also the first Jewish woman to become a judge there. She ended up working in that role until the end of her life.

Ruth was a well-respected and loved judge. She made lots of changes to the legal system that helped girls and women. And, in the end, some of the people she'd fought against realized she'd been right, and ended up helping her!

Ruth not only began changing the laws on equality during her lifetime, but also changed other people's minds, too. All rise for the honorable Judge RBG!

To better understand what Ruth did as a judge, let's try some courtroom roleplay!

We're going to discover the world of law. In our scenario, the cat took the gold fish's favorite toy.

1. Turn your living room into a courtroom by creating a jury box with pillows. Then, get a seat for the witness stand. You can wear blankets as a judge's robe.
2. Decide who will be the judge. Two other people can be lawyers. And, of course, we need people to play the cat and the goldfish, too!
3. Begin the trial! First, both lawyers will need to tell the judge why they think their party (fish or cat) is innocent or guilty. Then, you'll interview the cat and fish themselves to try and discover the truth. At the end, the judge will decide what happens!

15
TONI MORRISON

Author & Editor | Fiction | Goddess of Storytelling
Champion of Afro-American

February 18, 1931 – August 5, 2019

Lorain, Ohio

*"If there's a book that you want to read, but it
hasn't been written yet, then you must write it."*

Toni Morrison looked at the little girl at the front of the class with a caring smile. She was giving a presentation on writing at her son's school.

"I've said it time and time again—if there's a book you want to read, but it does not exist, then you must be the one to write it. This is why I write stories from my perspective, and mine alone. I write what I feel needs to come out of me."

The little girl, along with the other students in her class, began smiling.

"You'll always hear the writing advice 'write what you know.' Well—" Toni put her hands on her hips and looked at the students with a stern eye. She looked at her son in the back. He was smiling. "As a single mother who raised two boys, worked her butt off, and wrote when my boys were sleeping, you better believe I wrote stories about not getting dessert."

Everyone laughed.

Toni shook her head and walked over to the blackboard. "No, that's not true...I wrote about homework not being done." Another laugh. Toni picked up the chalk and began writing. "The truth is, I can tell you without a shadow of a doubt that I don't care what anyone else thinks of my books. I do it for me."

This is what she put on the board. "I do it for me" was written in large capital letters.

"And you should, too. Tell the stories you want to hear. Then, once you've done that," she said, turning back and smiling, "tell 'em again."

The class burst into applause and Toni winked at her son in the back, who was smiling with pride.

Toni had the great skill of giving beautiful answers to simple questions. This stemmed from the fact that she knew herself. But what does that mean? Well, who are you, beyond your name? What hobbies do you like, and what makes you unique? If your personality was a great, undiscovered land, what would it look like?

Toni Morrison was an author who wrote novels about the African-American experience in America. She was a trailblazer in the publishing world of African-American and Black fiction. She was also a great speaker on the philosophy of her ideas, as well as a writing teacher.

But as serious as her work was, she was always a joyous and happy person! She believed humor was a way to look at humanity evenly. It was a torch in the dark that helped us to see clearly. It was also a way she made people feel relaxed with her work. Finally, she knew that it was a good way to get to know ourselves a little better.

Toni's love of books and stories began at a young age. She loved visiting worlds where anything was possible. But, as she got older, she noticed a missing voice in all of the books she was reading: There weren't enough Black and African-American authors telling their stories.

Book publishing in America in the 1940s, '50s, and '60s was mostly books written by White men. So, when stories by African-American authors and many other authors of color began appearing, Toni was overjoyed. She wanted to see more of it, and wanted to help that happen, so she began trying to work in publishing.

Toni realized that, without any training, she would have a tough time getting a job. So she enrolled at university and earned a degree in writing and teaching. If she couldn't work in publishing, then she thought that she could perhaps teach others how to write.

Even with her degree, it was hard for an African-American woman to get a job in publishing. It was even harder because she was a single mother with two boys. She was busy being a parent. But Toni stayed strong and fearless. She found another way. Toni used her teaching degree to teach, and eventually got a job as a textbook editor for one of Random House's (a big publisher) smaller publishers. From there, she began searching out authors she knew deserved more attention. She was in!

But, that's not all... As one of the first female African-American editors to work for the big publishing houses, Toni was helping change the world. Her vision was that African-American authors, and any other minority author, should be as popular as any White author. She wanted their work to be accessible everywhere.

While Toni had been championing other writers, she had continued writing her own stories, too. In 1970, she released her first book. It was called *The Bluest Eye*, and was about an African-American woman who wished she had blue eyes. The novel didn't really sell well, and people said racist things about it. But for Toni, it was a success. She stayed fearless and didn't listen to those silly ideas. The people who had actually read the book knew how groundbreaking it truly was.

For the next 17 years, this was Toni's life—writing books and helping others write them, too. She knew who she was and why she was on her crusade to publish. She was inspiring Black women to tell their stories.

Then she wrote *Beloved*, and everything changed.

Beloved was a sensation! It was her most successful book and talked about a lot of important topics in America's history with racism. Pretty much everyone agreed how great it was. Toni won lots of awards, including the Pulitzer Prize for fiction. This made her a legend, and made the book very popular. Most importantly, it turned a sad chapter of America's history into an opportunity for others to learn!

What's more, the book was loved by another fearless girl in this book (Oprah), who told everyone on her show about it. Soon, everyone was reading *Beloved* and learning of this sad tale that Toni had told, which brought peace and understanding to many.

Tony believed that understanding each other was what we truly passed on—that was what real wisdom was. That was why she wrote books and helped others write them, too.

Toni Morrison was a prolific writer, and lots of people have found strength in her words. Here are five favorite quotes for you to enjoy!

1. "All water has a perfect memory and is forever trying to get back to where it was."
2. "Make a difference about something other than yourselves."
3. "I wrote my first novel because I wanted to read it."
4. "My children are delightful people, whom I would love even if they weren't my children."
5. "I would solve a lot of literary problems just thinking about a character in the subway, where you can't do anything anyway."

16
JANET GUTHRIE

Female NASCAR Driver | Aerospace Engineer
Gal Born to Drive

March 7, 1938 – Present

Iowa City, Iowa

*"Racing takes everything you've got—intellectually,
emotionally, physically—and then you have to
find about 10 percent more and use that, too."*

She saw it!

Janet Guthrie raced into the gap between the cars and overtook them both as they came around the bend.

Rooooooaaaarrrrr!!

She whooshed away from her opponents and moved into sixth place! The stretch before the next corner rocketed by her window. Janet was feeling amazing. She was a bit sick from all the car fumes, but she was too happy to care. Her cheeks hurt so much from smiling.

But she wasn't finished yet!

The Volunteer 400 was a big race, and she was the only woman racing in it!

Janet gripped the steering wheel and pulled as she banked the corner. It was really hard to drive at this speed! The car was trying to go straight, and she had to pull the steering wheel to keep it turning. Her arms hurt, and so did her hands, but she was sixth! She could massage her sore arms later.

A car roared up behind her and Janet pushed her accelerator. She changed gears and sped up. Now she was flying! It felt exactly like all the skydiving she'd done as a teenager.

She was 100 yards from the end.

50.

20.

10.

The joy bubbling in Janet's chest couldn't be contained! She whooped and cheered and laughed with happiness as she crossed the finish line. She'd just raced her best race.

She was flying with joy!

What makes you feel like you're flying? Is it when you're driving in a car or riding your bike? Have you ever gone fast in a car, like Janet?

In an era when women normally weren't even allowed in the pits of a NASCAR race, Janet Guthrie was breaking barriers by racing! The fact that she finished sixth in the Volunteer 400 was the stuff of legends.

Janet's competitors all drove lightweight, easily repairable cars with power steering, but Janet didn't have any of that. She drove a heavy "stock" car (like a basic racing car) with an even heavier engine…and it didn't have power steering, either!

But this didn't stop Janet. She was fearless and brave. She fought back against the sponsors and racers who said girls couldn't drive by showing them how great she truly was.

In only four seasons of racing NASCAR, she inspired generations of girls to dream beyond their expectations. Even if her career didn't go exactly as planned, she did some great things. She was the first woman to qualify for the Indianapolis and Daytona 500 races. She was also invited to race in the World 600—NASCAR's biggest race—and finished 15th, despite having a broken car! These races were already big deals in the racing world, but they became even bigger because a woman was racing. Millions of people saw Janet driving and proving her fantastic abilities in the races.

No matter where or when she raced, Janet proved how good she was by driving with skill and repairing her car with hard work and curiosity. She showed the world what women could do!

But, that's not all... Janet loved speed and adventure long before her racing days, thanks to her love of flying and skydiving.

Being the daughter of two pilots, Janet learned to fly a plane at 13. Then she learned skydiving at 16. There was nothing like it. From the pull of the control stick in her hands as she brought the plane into the air to the feeling of wind whipping against her cheeks as she plummeted towards the ground with her parachute strapped to her back, she was nothing if not adventurous.

Ever since she was a kid, Janet had known she wanted to be an adventurer—and she didn't think it was fair that only boys got to have all the fun.

Her real love of fun began when she bought her first car after college. Janet couldn't wait for the weekends, to go driving and speed along the hills and roads. She would turn tightly around the corners and overtake cars with ease, and loved fixing her car when it broke down. But Janet knew that treating the road like a racetrack was dangerous, and that she was being the wrong kind of adventurer.

That's when she found amateur racing.

Even though she was a girl, the other drivers on the local circuit didn't care. They were all there because they loved the sport of racing, and Janet was a natural behind the wheel, so she received a warm welcome.

The racetrack became her happy place. She could take the corners tighter, overtake quicker, and even go a lot faster! But racing like this meant she had to improve quickly. She had to have quick reaction times with her hands, and she had to concentrate and focus a lot longer. She would analyze the tracks and try to understand how they worked. "How sharp is the second corner?" "How long is that straight?" These were the questions she asked herself as a racing driver, and it was all this work that led her qualifying for NASCAR years later.

But racing wasn't always fair. Janet often talked about how unfair it was for women in the sport. Viewers liked seeing her on TV and fans loved seeing her in the stands, but sponsors didn't want to support her. After four seasons, Janet had to retire, as she could no longer afford to race. This saddened her for the rest of her life, but she was proud that she'd raced, regardless! And she never stopped racing or writing about racing after she retired from NASCAR.

Ultimately, her career created a lasting impact on the lives of the many little girls who'd seen her race. For Janet, that was the best win of all!

Janet loved going fast on the racetrack. To experience that speed, let's build a cardboard racetrack for toy cars!

What you'll need for this activity:

- Big cardboard box
- Longer piece of cardboard to make a ramp with
- Extra cardboard to create lanes
- Duct tape
- Utility knife or scissors (use with adult supervision)
- Ruler

Let's build!

1. Cut one side off of your big box—this way, you'll have three walls and an opening.
2. Place the long piece of cardboard in this opening. With the top edges lined up, cut to length and attach with tape.
3. Now, measure lanes to include on your track. It's easiest to divide the ramp into four equal lanes.
4. Measure and cut extra cardboard strips to make lanes (or, you can use straws and pipe cleaners). Remember to measure the lanes at least two inches shorter than the ramp so you can make a starting gate. Attach your lane dividers.
5. Cut another strip of cardboard to be used as a starting gate. This will be placed along the lanes, so make sure it's wider than the track (you'll pull it to release your cars).
6. Begin racing and having fun!
7. Optional step: Decorate your track and gate.

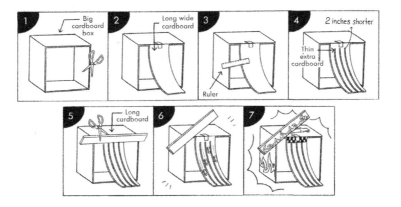

17
CONDOLEEZZA RICE

Secretary of State | Warrior Princess
Trailblazer of Leadership
October 20, 1964 – Present
Oakland, California

*"The day has to come when it's not a surprise that
a woman has a powerful position."*

"We must be careful," Condoleezza Rice said. She looked out at the room of academic scholars, professors, and arms control experts. All of these important people were gathered at Stanford University for a CISAC meeting—the Center for International Security and Cooperation. They were talking about something really serious, but also really dangerous: nuclear weapons.

As a scholarship student of political science, Condoleezza was giving a speech about what she'd been studying. But in a room full of White men, there were only three other women—and she was the only African-American woman!

Condoleezza nodded at her friends.

"We've talked a lot about what's happening in the world at the moment, and how it could affect us. But I believe we've forgotten the most important thing, which is staying safe."

Condoleezza felt less nervous the more she spoke. She just tried not to think of who she was talking to. President Ford's last national security advisor was there!

"We need to be careful how we handle this 'cold war.' It's 1985, and the world has changed a lot since it started. What might seem like winning for America could be defense for others. We are a young country compared to many. And just as young people tend to do, we think we know it all." Condoleezza smiled and a few of the people in the audience chuckled.

"But the United States doesn't know everything—which doesn't necessarily mean we're in danger. Acting without understanding the whole picture would be dangerous. I believe we can end this conflict by building friendships and showing kindness. We're different, but both communism and democracy want people to be safe. We need to see how we're similar, instead of focusing on what makes us different. That will be how we truly win."

The men in the room began clapping. Condoleezza accepted the applause with a smile and continued speaking.

"Now, with my introduction out of the way, let's begin unpacking this idea of safety and understanding others.

Are you interested in learning about the rest of the world? Condoleezza was fascinated by how the world governments worked, and that's why she became a political scientist. How do you think countries can remain friends and help each other?

If negotiating was an Olympic event, Condoleezza Rice would have won golds throughout her career!

Condoleezza didn't know it at the time, but the speech and passion she showed at the 1985 CISAC meeting impressed a lot of people—most importantly Brent Scowcroft. Brent had been President Ford's national security advisor. After the meeting, he offered to mentor her, because he believed she was incredible. Then, when President George H. Bush was elected, Brent returned to his advising role with the president— except this time, he brought Condoleezza!

This was the beginning of Condoleezza's super negotiating career.

Along with being America's first African-American secretary of state, Condoleezza's skilled negotiating and advising meant she helped lots of different presidents of the United States. The heart of her negotiating skills lay in being honest, friendly, and caring.

During her time as secretary of state, Condoleezza traveled the most miles any secretary of state had ever traveled! She flew all over the world, meeting politicians, presidents, women, men, and children from all walks of life. She believed it was her duty to make as many friends as possible for America, throughout the world.

This is why so many presidents asked her for help. She just cared so much about understanding the world, which helped during negotiations and talks between countries.

From talks with Russia in the late 1980s and early 1990s to befriending many officials and politicians in the Middle East during the Iraq War, Condoleezza's way of working was effective. Understanding other nations and being friends with them and respectful of their beliefs was how she could do so much good! She created friendships and allies for the US, even if they were on the other side of the world.

But that's not all... Condoleezza's confidence and self-belief didn't necessarily make things easy all the time. Some people didn't like women being involved with politics or important issues, especially African-American women.

However, the issues Condoleezza wanted to discuss were just too important. She'd dealt with racism as a child and knew how small it had made her feel. This fueled her passion to improve things. Through powerful speeches and peaceful protesting, she helped shape a brighter future for all African-Americans.

When Condoleezza began helping the US Government during the 1980s, she was often the only woman in the room. Her ideas were often dismissed because of her gender, and she wasn't taken as seriously as a man would have been. But she didn't let this stop her. Instead, she saw it as a challenge to work smarter and strategize more effectively. She fought sexism with her intelligence and determination. She studied more, read more, and practiced more. She refused to be seen as the "new girl" who could be walked over. With hard work, she made sure she was ready for any argument. She didn't always win, but she was always prepared. Soon, everyone realized it didn't matter that she was a woman, she was just too good!

Condoleezza becoming the 66th Secretary of State of the United States of America was proof of what fearlessness could achieve. There were many peaceful warriors in America effecting change by listening and making themselves heard. Not too many years before, during Condoleezza's childhood, she'd lived under Black and White segregation. Now, here she was in the White House!

Condoleezza Rice has achieved a lot of great things in her life, and she believes the hurdles she overcame made it possible for her to do so. Fighting racism and sexism made her stronger, and she hopes all girls can be inspired by her story.

Condoleezza has certainly achieved a lot in her life.
But she's more than an educator and politician.
Here are five cool facts about her.

1. Condoleezza is a really good piano player. She almost became a concert pianist before deciding to work in politics!
2. Condoleezza is also a huge sports fan. Her favorite sports are football and figure skating.
3. She's also an accomplished athlete, herself. She's a black belt in taekwondo, and has run many marathons.
4. Condoleezza can speak four languages! She's really good at English, Russian, French, and Spanish.
5. Finally, Condoleezza is a huge Star Trek fan. She loves the show's exploration of life, science, politics, and ideas.

18
ROBERTA
"BOBBI" GIBB

Marathon Runner | Lawyer & Artist
Running with the Wind
November 2, 1942 – Present
Cambridge, Massachusetts

"I ran the Boston Marathon out of love. I believe that love is the basis of all meaningful human endeavors. Yet it was a love that was incomplete until it was shared with others."

Roberta "Bobbi" Gibb's hands were shaking!

She was standing by her mailbox, unable to go inside because of what she held in her hands. It was a letter about running in the Boston Marathon!

She'd been training for years. She'd run lots of miles and practiced as much as she could. Applying to run in the prestigious marathon had been easy, but now opening the letter seemed so hard.

Bobbi felt unsure. She knew people still had funny ideas about women running, but she wanted to prove them wrong.

She gulped and ripped open the letter. She had to know.

Bobbi began reading, but from the first line she knew she wasn't going to be allowed to run. Reading to the end confirmed it. They didn't want her to run.

It was so unfair! Her stomach clenched. She was so sad that she wanted to just sit down by the mailbox.

All that training, wasted. All those cold mornings running in her sweatshirt—

Suddenly, Bobbi had an idea.

She couldn't believe she hadn't considered it. She would still run—and picturing herself running made her laugh. She would wear her brother's sweatshirt and pants. No one would suspect a girl was running in a boys' race in those stinky clothes!

What's the furthest you've ever run? Would you like to run as far as Bobbi? If you wanted to start running as an activity, how would you start? Would you join a club, or see if you could run for your school?

Running takes guts and lots of training—and for Bobbi in 1966, it also took a disguise! Luckily, you don't have to wear a disguise now if you want to run, but back then, Bobbi had to. It was the only way she could get into the race.

Bobbi refused to give up on her goal of running the Boston Marathon. She loved running and competing, so she committed herself to sneaking into the race disguised as her brother.

Bobbi didn't even live in Boston! She had to travel for two nights and three days (all on a bus) to run the race. But on April 19th, 1966, that is exactly what she did!

As silly as it sounds, back then, Bobbi wasn't allowed to run the race because she was a girl. The officials wouldn't even allow women in the starting area (in case they tried to run). So. Bobbi hid in the bushes near the starting line and waited for the race to start. When half the runners had begun, she jumped from the bushes and started running. She passed by all the judges and officials in her disguise. Then, when she was off and going, she pulled off her hood and ran freely.

She was in the middle of the pack, and there was no turning back! And, as it turned out, everyone was so welcoming! The men loved that a woman was running with them.

And so Bobbi ran.

Some people change the world throughout the course of their lives, and some people change the world in an instant. For Bobbi, she changed the world in 3 hours, 21 minutes, and 40 seconds, which is how long it took her to complete the Boston Marathon.

Bobbie's run was a hugely inspirational moment for all girls and women. For a long time, men had dominated the sport of running, and it had been the men who decided women couldn't run that far. But Bobbi easily proved them wrong.

Instead of everyone booing (which is what she'd been told would happen in the letter), they cheered her on the whole way. By the time she got to the finish line, it had become big news that a girl was running the race—so big that Governor John Volpe came out and shook her hand! He was proud of her for running the race. In fact, the only person who was angry she'd run was the man who'd sent her the rude letter!

But, that's not all... Bobbi ran the Boston Marathon again in 1967!

And then again in 1968!

For as long as she could, Bobbi kept running marathons. Each day, she reminded people what was possible. She also reminded them never to let someone else tell them their limit.

Bobbi continued running marathons, but now she was running with other women! So many women were running marathons, they had to create specific women's marathons. So much for girls not being able to do it!

Bobbi's belief in her running ability had helped her train all those years in solitude. Later, that same self-belief helped her become a lawyer and creative artist, too, which ended up bringing her running career full circle..

During the 1984 Olympic trials, marathon events were now being held for women. Because Bobbi had been so inspiring years earlier, the committee wanted to involve her. Knowing that she was also an accomplished artist and sculptor, the committee asked her to make three unique statues for the three winners! How cool is that?

Bobbi knew it was special, so she made the best statues she could. Each statue was unique and celebrated the women receiving them.

Bobbi still inspires runners today! On the 50th anniversary of her protesting marathon, they invited her back to run it again...and she did! For 50 years, she had remained fearless, and everyone that followed learned how to run from her.

What really helped Bobbi Gibb run her marathon was the fact that she believed in herself! The best way to learn to believe in ourselves is with affirmations. Here are five more affirmations to recite daily.

1. "I believe in myself."
2. "I can do hard things."
3. "I am strong."
4. "I compete only with myself."
5. "I am capable of great things."

19
DOROTHY ARZNER

Film Director | Editor and Scriptwriter
Trailblazer Behind the Camera
January 3, 1897 – October 1, 1979
San Francisco, California

*"When I went to work in a studio, I took my pride
and made a nice little ball of it and threw
it right out the window."*

"Cut!" Dorothy Arzner called.

Everyone relaxed and the set became a buzz of noise. No one was more excited than Dorothy, because she was directing! It was huge. But she had to remain cool...the producer was coming over!

"Great stuff, Dorothy," he said. He'd been watching from just off to the side of the set. "You've saved us here."

"More than happy to help!" Dorothy said. "It should all blend in pretty well. Our stock footage of bullfights is pretty exciting."

"And you were pretty good with directing, too," the producer added. "Editing lets you see all the angles.

"Thanks. Let's hope there's more to come."

"You know what, I hope so, too," the producer said, smiling. "Let me speak to some people. If this works out, maybe there's more we can do together."

Dorothy nodded and turned away to continue working. She finally allowed herself to smile. She was ecstatic. There weren't many women directing in Hollywood in 1922—if any! The fact that she was directing all these scenes today was huge.

Would you like to be a film director? If you were going to tell a story through film, what would you pick? Do you have any favorite fairy tales you would like to see as a movie?

With one great idea, Dorothy Arzner's life changed! She went from being behind the film and editing to being behind the camera and directing—in an instant! It was a huge win for girls everywhere!

Before movies had sound and color, they were black and white and had no sound. Characters would speak on the screen with no sound, then a new shot with text would be shown (kind of like funny subtitles). The movies were still exciting, and still a lot of fun to make and see, but they were silent!

Blood and Sand was a silent film from 1927 made by Paramount Pictures. It told the story of a famous bullfighter's downfall. But, unlike today, when movie studios can make super exciting bullfights with CGI or recreate them realistically, Paramount didn't have the money or technology to do that. Fortunately, Dorothy's knowledge of editing and what footage they had in storage allowed her to solve their problem. They could still have an exciting end to their movie!

Even though Dorothy directed some of the bullfighting scenes for *Blood and Sand*, she was not credited for them. Back then, the main director was credited with directing all scenes, even if someone else had done it. But for Dorothy, it was a chance to show Paramount her skills—and they were impressed. It made them wonder what she could achieve if she was directing full time. She had the knowledge, so they gave her the opportunity.

Dorothy showed them! She was the first woman to direct a sound film (in 1929) and the first female director to join the Directors Guild of America (a group that represents working film directors). Trailblazing was practically Dorothy's middle name. In fact, for a long time, she was the only woman directing feature films in Hollywood!

Her huge career as a director stretched from 1927 to 1943, and during those years she directed 20 films. She also launched the careers of famous actresses like Katherine Hepburn, Rosalind Russell, and Lucille Ball (all fearless women in their own right)!

But, that's not all... While Dorothy would go on to become a revolutionary female director, in the beginning, she had dreams of being a doctor. Film only became an interest when she realized she hated blood! Luckily, a friend introduced her to a friend who was a director—and that's where Dorothy found her calling.

Hollywood was booming in the early 1900s, and Dorothy's friend was a director named William DeMille, who worked for Paramount Studios. DeMille liked Dorothy and thought she could be good in film. Since Dorothy didn't really know what she wanted to do, DeMille's assistant told her to start with typing scripts. That way, she'd at least know what the film was about.

Dorothy loved creating stories and writing about people's lives. She was so good at it that Paramount promoted her to being an editor. Back then, editing involved physically cutting and repairing the tape they filmed on.

Her experience editing was what helped save the day during the filming of *Blood and Sand* all those years later. Because Dorothy had spent so much time cutting and repairing film tape, she saw movies differently. She wondered how shots could be filmed in new ways. What if they made people look differently with shadows, or made them look small by showing more of a background? Dorothy wanted to tell stories with the movie scenes themselves, along with the narratives she'd written. Today, this has become common practice in Hollywood.

Once Dorothy started filming movies with sound, she grew frustrated with sound problems. She even developed the boom mic to better capture sound on set (this is a microphone on the end of a *reaaaaally* long stick that hangs above actors when they talk).

Like any true trailblazer, Dorothy's path wasn't without its challenges. She was a female director during a time when Hollywood was still making silly rules about its films and crew. They began to heavily censor what they thought was right or appropriate. Soon, Dorothy had trouble finding funding for films, which was even more annoying when plenty of other, less-talented male directors found money easily. Despite this, Dorothy created films with strong female leads and always defied expectations. Her motto was that she would be so good they couldn't ignore her—and she was!

Sadly, Hollywood made a rule in the 1940s that stopped all women directors from working. This angered Dorothy, but there was nothing she could do. So she adapted and began teaching. She decided she would pave a way for future directors by inspiring her students to break the trends set by Hollywood. They should film what they truly wanted to see. One of those students was Francis Ford Coppola, who went on to become a legendary filmmaker.

Dorothy's fearlessness and strong self-belief allowed her to create an amazing life in film. She wrote, edited, and directed groundbreaking films that changed her life and the lives of many others. Her biggest skill was being interested in every stage of the filmmaking process, because she never knew when that knowledge would come in handy. Maybe it is time someone made a film about her!

Can you imagine films as vividly as Dorothy did?
The best way to see what's in your mind is to practice,
so let's make a shoebox set!

For this activity, you'll need:

- A shoebox
- Little figurines
- Sticky tape
- Glue
- Scissors

- Colored pencils and pens
- Card and cardboard to make furniture or buildings

Let's make your set!

1. Imagine you're making a film and telling a story. Think about your characters and where the story is taking place. What's happening?
2. You can either turn your shoebox sideways, so that you have a "roof" on your set, or you can cut one panel off the box so there's "sky" on your set.
3. Once you decide whether your set has a roof or sky, begin building your vision and story.
4. Place set pieces and furniture around the set, as well as your little figurines.
5. Pretend you're the director and shoot your movie!

20
HEDY LAMARR

Actress & Inventor | Lover of Privacy
Goddess of the Invisible Waves
November 9, 1914 – January 19, 2000
Vienna, Austria

"Hope and curiosity about the future seemed better than guarantees. That's the way I was. The unknown was always so attractive to me...and still is."

"There. Now, connect those cables," Hedy Lamarr's father said. Hedy and her father were sitting in his study, making a radio. She'd never made a radio before—or anything, for that matter. This was her first time inventing or making something, but her father was showing her how easy it was.

"Now, let's put the case on." Hedy's father picked up the shell and placed it over the many wires, filaments, conductors, and glowing tubes. It all looked like magic to Hedy.

She was giddy as he placed it down carefully. Her hands tingled as if electricity were running through her.

"Now, connect the plug."

Hedy inserted the plug into the wall.

"Switch it on."

Hedy switched the radio on by turning the dial. *Whoommmbbb!* The radio came to life! It began crackling and screeching immediately. "It works!" she called out.

"Of course," her father laughed. "Now, let's tune it." He wound the knob until some music came on. Once the radio was tuned in, her father took Hedy's hand and they began dancing in his small study.

They waltzed in a circle and Hedy felt so happy. "I can't believe how easy that was."

Her father smiled. "It's easy when you understand how things work. You should always strive to understand, Hedy. Science—and applied science, at that—is all about problem solving. And how do we solve a problem?"

"We understand it. We define it," she replied.

"Exactly." He smiled. "Beautiful, isn't it?" They looked at the radio. "An invention so simple, yet so magical. The best ones are like that. Magical. Invisible. Unseen."

Hedy couldn't stop smiling as they listened and danced to the music. Today was one of the best days of her life!

Sometimes, inventions solve problems we don't even know we have! Ask a friend or parent what problem they have. Could you invent something to help them with it?

We can only imagine how much Hedy and her father played with science together, but what an impact their curiosity had on her life. Hedy viewed science and invention as a way to play. She loved solving problems in unexpected ways.

It was this sense of play and invention that Hedy enjoyed in acting, too. Growing up in Austria, she felt she was close to many historical breakthroughs. But as much as she enjoyed science, it was acting that brought Hedy to the world's attention. While she began her career in Berlin, it was in Hollywood where she became a megastar.

Acting in Hollywood during the 1940s and 1950s was exciting. Hedy got to work with famous directors and actors, visit beautiful places, and meet adoring fans.

But acting for Hedy also meant something else....

For her, acting meant she could spend money on science and inventing! The whole time she'd been acting, the joy of science and invention had never left her. In fact, Hedy refused to stop tinkering and coming up with ideas—even on set. She always kept a science journal with her to read. She wanted to know everything about the world of science and inventing, because she was bursting with ideas. She wanted to help make the world a better place.

Before Hedy's biggest invention came into being, she invented lots of small things that had big effects on society. From dissolving tablets that made fizzy soda drinks to tastier stock cubes for cooking, Hedy was always trying to create things that could make people's lives easier. She even had an idea to create a radio-controlled traffic light that changed when cars were near! That idea also led to her next invention....

Hedy thought there was something interesting about radio waves, but she wasn't sure what it was...yet! She knew she would figure it out if she kept being curious.

Of course, being a curious woman sometimes led to trouble. Men often failed to take her seriously and thought she was joking. They couldn't believe that a woman would like science—let alone be an inventor! But Hedy just ignored them and their harsh words. She was too busy inventing.

But, that's not all... Hedy's greatest idea came during a time when many other women showed that they were superheroes—World War II.

Hedy loved her new home country of America, and wanted to help out and be useful. During all her years as an inventor and reading scientific journals, the importance of radio had always been talked about. Radio-guided *anything* was the big idea a lot of people wanted to solve. But there was one big problem: Radio signals could be blocked and tracked, which could potentially prevent messages from being sent or received. No one could figure out how to solve this problem, until Hedy.

One night, Hedy was talking about the big radio problem with a friend who played piano. As radio had become really important in World War II, Hedy was determined to solve the problem. She wanted to keep soldiers safe and stop signals from getting blocked. While playing piano, she got her idea.

Hedy noticed that piano keys jumped from one sound to another instantly. You could go from one to the other with just your hands. But with radios, you had to fiddle with knobs and frequencies to get anywhere!

What if you could "jump" between radio frequencies like the piano keys, she thought? What if you could switch frequencies with the press of a button? Hedy thought this could stop radios from being blocked, so she began studying her idea scientifically, and eventually took it to the US Navy to test.

This idea was pretty cool, and the US Navy really liked it. But they didn't know what to do with it, or how to use it. It actually took them years to figure out how to use it, as it was a really smart idea and no technology existed that could do it! But soon the world understood the idea Hedy had invented, and technology was able to do what she had thought of.

Hedy's idea of using radio waves like this became the basis of a lot of inventions that are now commonplace in our world, including Wi-Fi,

Bluetooth, GPS, and even how smartphones communicate with the world—all because she was curious and wanted to help improve the world.

Every day, when you log on to a Wi-Fi signal, think of Hedy and how she loved science and inventing things. Think of how she used her skill to fuel her passion. As it turns out, sometimes what we love doesn't have to be what we do for work!

Hedy's breakthrough for her pre-Wi-Fi invention had to do with radio and soundwaves. A great way to understand a soundwave is with a tin-can walkie talkie!

This activity shows a physical representation of invisible soundwaves. Everything we hear is made of invisible waves, and radio and Wi-Fi work with invisible waves, too.

What you'll need:

- Two washed tin cans
- A hammer + nail
- Length of string

Ready? *Kssht! Over!*

1. Turn both cans upside down and bang the nail through the end of one of your tin cans. Remove and repeat on the second can.
2. Place the ends of the string through each tin can, so that the bottoms of each tin can are facing towards each other. Tie knots at the ends of each string so that they can't slide through the holes made by the nail.

3. Have each kid walk apart until the string is tight. One kid can talk while the other listens. Voila! You've got a quick and easy walkie talkie!

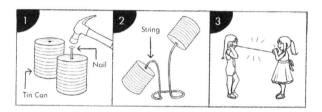

Made in the USA
Middletown, DE
19 September 2024

61128512R00070